CONTE

4	MEET 1D	50	MIX PICS
6	GIVE US A BREAK	52	DREAM DAYS
8	WILD ABOUT HARRY	54	VA VA VIDEO
10	NUTS FOR NIALL	56	PRANK-STARS
12	LOOPY FOR LIAM	58	SPOT THE DIFFERENCE
14	CRAZY FOR ZAYN	60	HARRY: QUICK QUIZ
16	LOVIN' LOUIS	62	MISSING LYRICS
18	STAR SIGNS	64	ON THE COVER
20	WHAT'S IN A NAME	66	LOUIS: QUICK QUIZ
22	TWISTED LYRICS	68	LOOK LIVELY!
24	TWEET, TWEET	70	PHONE A FRIEND
26	FACE RACE	72	ZAYN: QUICK QUIZ
28	STAR QUOTES	74	STARRY QUOTES
30	ALRIGHT, PET?	76	PET PUZZLER
32	CROSSWORD	78	LIAM: QUIZ
34	POSTER PAGE	80	BRAIN TEASER
36	YOU'RE THE BEST	82	SPORTS DAY
38	WHO WORE IT?	84	TREE OF FRIENDS
40	1D WARDROBE	86	SPOT THE DIFFERENCE
42	UP ALL NIGHT	88	NIALL: QUICK QUIZ
44	WHAT GOES ON TOUR...	90	KEY CHAINS
46	BUBBLE BANTER	92	THE TRICKY SIX
48	WORDSEARCH	94	ANSWERS

MEET 1D ONE DIRECTION

They were five ordinary boys, living ordinary lives in an ordinary town near you. But despite different backgrounds and upbringings, they shared musical talent, determination and one dream - to make it in the music industry. And boy, have they made it. In the past two years, One Direction's achievements have already surpassed their wildest imaginings. From talent show beginnings as would-be solo artists, the boys have gone on to become the UK's most successful boy-band, managing to crack the American market. With a number one album, three hit singles, two books and a sell-out tour under their belt; it's no wonder fans around the globe just can't get enough of 1D.

Here's where you swear your allegiance to the lads and test your knowledge of all things 1D in our amazing quiz book, which looks into every aspect of the lads' lives. So pick up a pen and point it in the right direction.

My name is   and I'm a true Directioner.
....

QUICK TRIV:
Which band member thought up the group's name?

GIVE US A BREAK

The boys are all so talented that they were always destined for greatness. Harry was the lead singer of a band, Liam, Zayn and Niall were showing early vocal promise and Louis was acting. Then *The X Factor* gave them the platform to shine and they've never looked back.

THE FIRST STEP

ZAYN
"My music teacher suggested that I went for it. I first got an application form when I was 15, but I chickened out and didn't fill it in. I did the same the following year, but when I was 17 I was finally brave enough."

NIALL
"I'd always known I wanted to give *The X Factor* a go… (Former contestant) Lloyd Daniels said 'I told you to go for it'. But he actually didn't."

LOUIS
"In 2009 I applied but didn't get through the first round… When I tried out the second time I was more driven than ever."

LIAM
"I was 14 when I first tried out for *The X Factor*. It was horrible to be turned away at the judges houses, but if I had made the live shows I wouldn't have known what had hit me…. When I was 16, I decided to give *The X Factor* another go."

HARRY
"I didn't know if I had what it took and I was really nervous about actually applying, so in the end my mum filled out the form and sent it off for me."

SING IT LOUD

Can you name the song that each of the lads performed at their first audition?

Liam sang... *thats wat makes you Butiful*
Zayn sang...
Harry sang...
Niall sang...
Louis sang...

NEVER FORGET

Guess which band member each memory belongs to, then write the correct number in each box...

A. "At bootcamp, I had a photo taken with Harry because I knew he was going to be famous. I even gave him a hug and told him not to worry because I knew he'd be fine."

B. "That trip to Spain (to the Judges houses) was the first time I'd been abroad."

C. "Apart from the other lads I got on best with Rebecca and Matt and I still get on really well with them now."

D. "I have so many great memories of being in the house, especially all of the times I went naked. Sometimes I was totally starkers and sometimes I wore a thong."

E. "Our room was so bad that one day when we all went out for work, Esther from Belle Amie cleaned it for us because she found it so horrific."

WILD ABOUT HARRY

Who can resist his unruly mop of curls and cheeky grin? Time to kick it with the lad from up North!

NAME: Harry Edward Styles
NICKNAMES: 'Hazza', 'H', 'Curls' or 'Potter'
D.O.B: 1 February 1994
STAR SIGN: Aquarius
FAVE COLOUR: Blue
FROM: Holmes Chapel, Cheshire

HARRY'S BEST...

ALBUM: '21' by Adele
BODY PART: My hands – they're soft
GRUB: Sweetcorn
FRIEND FOREVER: Louis Tomlinson
STORE: Selfridges
MOBILE APP: Texts From Last Night
TV SHOW: Family Guy
WAY TO CHILLAX: Getting massages – I've always had a bad back
NIGHT OUT: Going for dinner with mates
BAND: The Beatles, Queen

SCHOOL DAYS
Harry attended Holmes Chapel Comprehensive School. He enjoyed maths and P.E. and worked hard, although he often got told off for talking in class.

EARLY PROMISE
Harry appeared in several school productions and once played Buzz Lightyear in *Chitty Chitty Bang Bang*.

I'M IN THE BAND
Before 1D, Harry was lead singer in a band called White Eskimo with school friends Will, Hayden and Nick. They sang Bryan Adams' track 'Summer of 69' in a school competition and won and were asked to perform at the wedding of a school friend's mum. A record producer who was a guest at the wedding said they were good and told Harry he looked like a young Mick Jagger!

GIRLS, GIRLS, GIRLS.
- Aged just 12, Harry went steady with a school friend called Emilie. They are still good friends but he names his first serious girlfriend as "a girl called Abi".
- When it comes to the ladeez, Harry doesn't have a 'type'. He likes girls he can talk to and who could get on with his family.
- His celeb crush is Frankie Sandford of The Saturdays.

YOUTHFUL HAUNTS
Great Budworth Ice Cream Farm in Cheshire. Harry and his friend Reg used to cycle there daily during the summer holidays and he even took the 1D boys there during *The X Factor* process.

Harry

NUTS FOR NIALL

He may be the youngest member of the group, but he's every bit as talented. Read on for the low-down on the cute blonde with the Irish charm.

NAME: Niall James Horan
NICKNAMES: 'Nialler'
D.O.B: 13 September 1993
STAR SIGN: Virgo
FAVE COLOUR: Purple
FROM: Mullingar, Ireland

NIALL'S BEST...

ALBUM: 'Crazy Love' by Michael Bublé
BODY PART: My eyes
GRUB: Sweetcorn
FRIEND FOREVER: Sean, Scott, Dillan and Brad – mates from Ireland
STORE: Topman
MOBILE APP: Flick Kick Football
TV SHOW: Two and A Half Men
WAY TO CHILLAX: Playing the guitar
NIGHT OUT: Hanging with mates
BAND: The Script, The Doors, Take That and West Life

SCHOOL DAYS
Niall was a popular pupil at Colaiste Mhuire boys' school. He loved french but hated maths. His teachers said he showed potential but seemed in a world of his own in class.

EARLY PROMISE
Niall loved singing from an early age. He was in the school choir and his auntie said she knew he would be famous from the moment she thought that Garth Brooks was on the radio, when in fact it was Niall singing. Niall loves the fact that his hero – Michael Bublé, had a similar childhood experience when his father thought his singing was the radio!

TALENT SHOW TALENT
By the time he auditioned for *The X Factor*, Niall was already a seasoned perfomer. From the age of 13 he'd taken part in local talent shows, singing everything from The Script's hit 'The Man Who Can't Be Moved' to Chris Brown's 'With You'.

GIRLS, GIRLS, GIRLS.
- Niall likes natural-looking, no-nonsense girls who like a laugh and can take a bit of banter. He says future girlfriends will "have to like football!"
- Niall has said his dream valentine date would be with Miranda Cosgrove who plays Carly in the TV show *iCarly*.
- His celeb crush is Cheryl Cole.

STUDENT DAYS
Niall's pre-1D plans involved going to university to study sound engineering. When he applied for *The X Factor* he was a student at St Mary CBS college and had begun studying for his leaving certificate (the Irish equivalent of A levels).

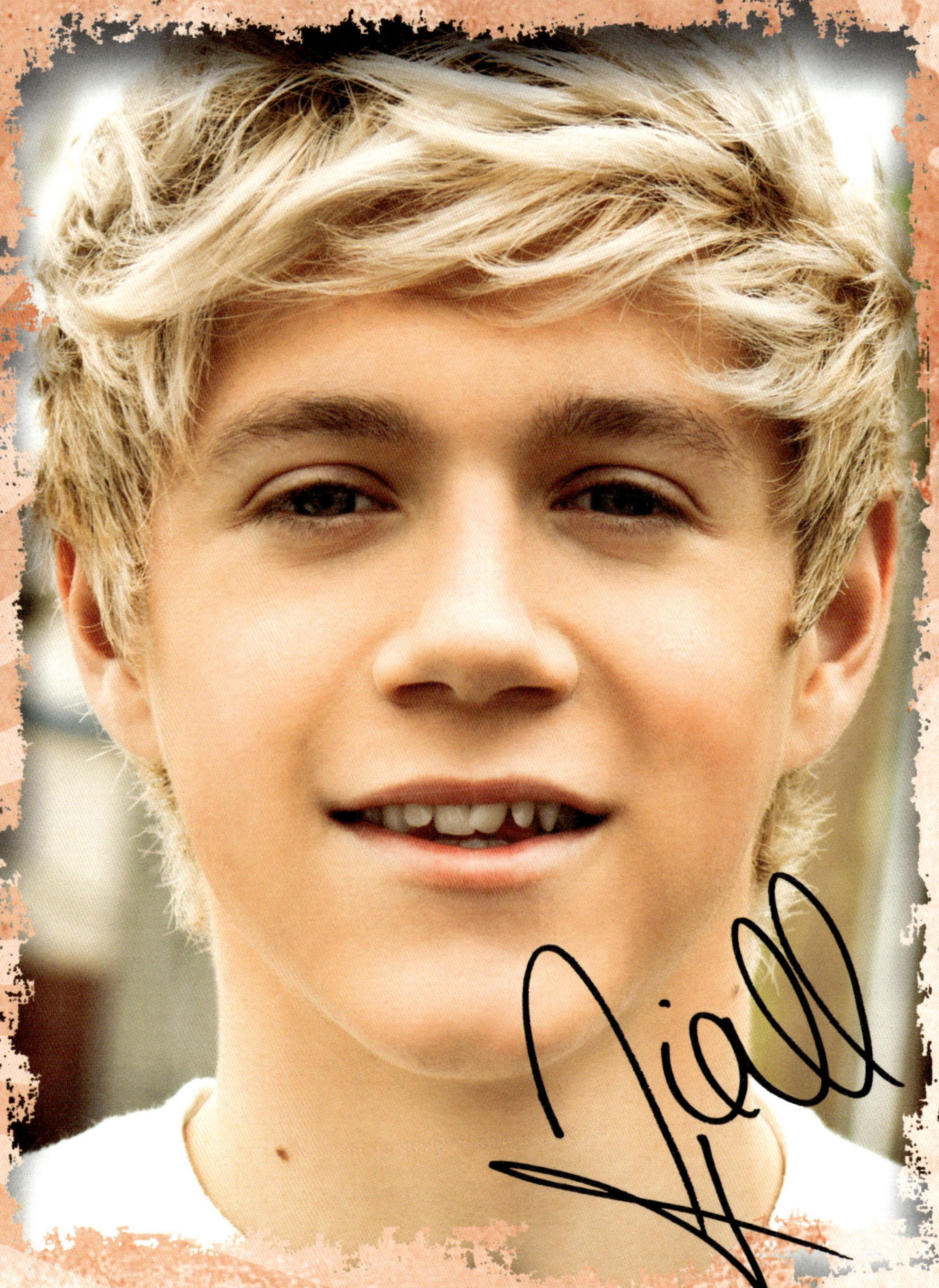
Niall

LOOPY FOR LIAM

Lovely Liam is just one of the lads, but he's got the voice of an angel and looks to match. Get ready to meet the man from the Midlands...

NAME: Liam James Payne
NICKNAMES: 'Lee', 'Paynee'
D.O.B: 29 August 1993
STAR SIGN: Virgo
FAVE COLOUR: Blue
FROM: Wolverhampton, West Midlands

LIAM'S BEST...

ALBUM: 'Echo' by Leona Lewis
BODY PART: My arms
GRUB: Chocolate
FRIEND FOREVER: Martin, Andy and Ronnie
STORE: All Saints
MOBILE APP: Flick Kick Football
TV SHOW: Friends and Everybody Loves Raymond
WAY TO CHILLAX: Staying in bed watching movies
NIGHT OUT: Bowling
BAND: One Republic

HEALTH SCARES
Liam was born three weeks early and was effectively still born, although doctors eventually managed to save him. He spent the first four years of his life in and out of hospital for tests before it was discovered that one of his kidneys doesn't function.

SCHOOL DAYS
Self-professed 'naughty boy' Liam found his niche at school when he discovered a talent for long distance running. He played basketball and even took up boxing aged 12 as a way to defend himself against bullies.

EARLY PROMISE
Liam joined the school choir in Year 9 and was part of a huge group of choirs which set a world record singing 'Lean on Me' in unison.

GIRLS, GIRLS, GIRLS
Liam likes curly girlies who are quiet but friendly. Sadly, he's already dating someone who fits all these criteria – backing dancer Danielle Peazer, who he's been seeing since 2010. His celeb crush is Leona Lewis.

WHEELER DEELER
Liam has an entrepreneurial streak and at school used to make around £50 a week bulk-buying sweets and selling them in the playground.

IN ANOTHER LIFE
Liam was so good at sport that his parents suggested he should go on to be a P.E. teacher.

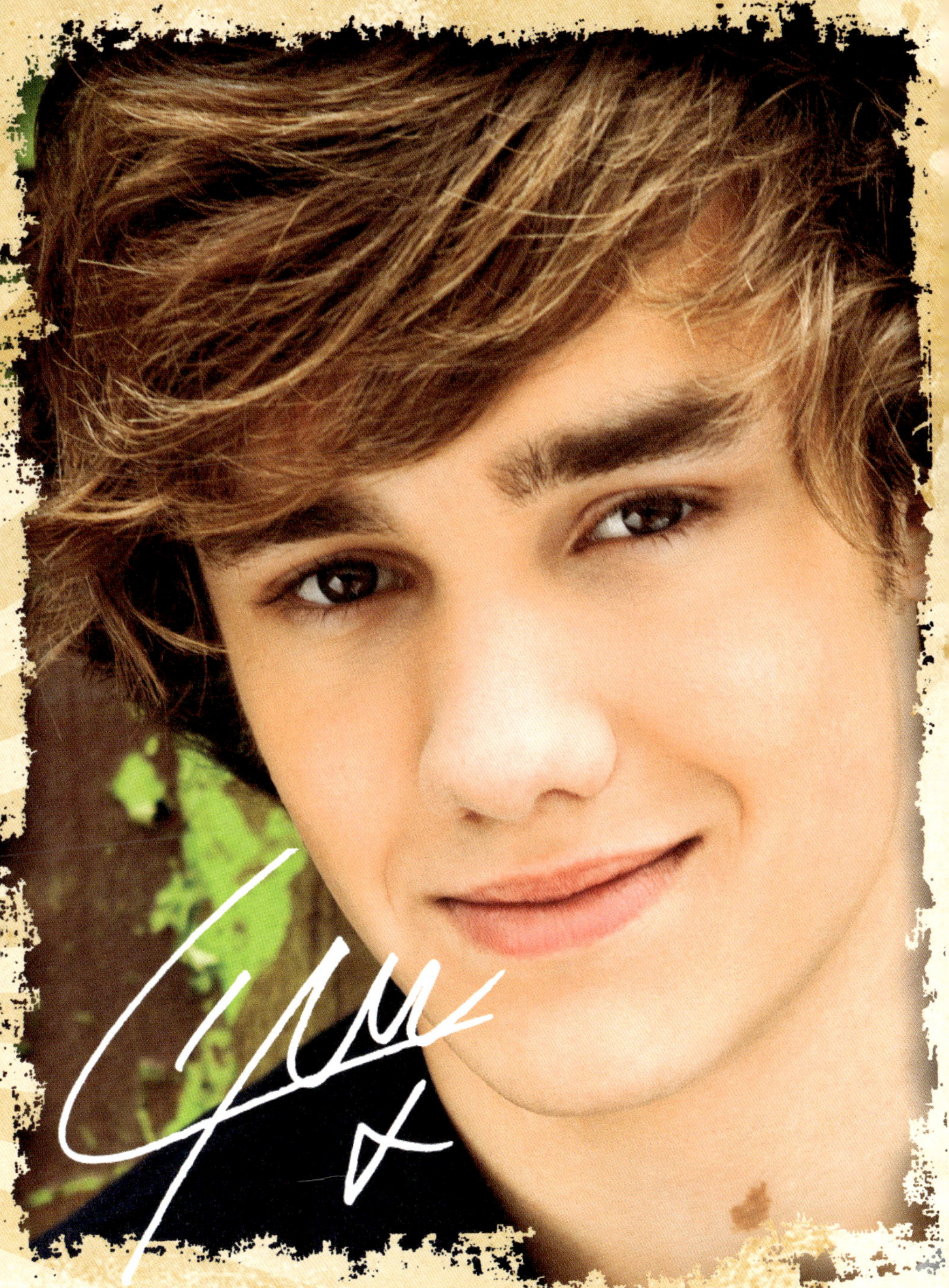

CRAZY FOR ZAYN

Does the mere sound of his name send you insane? If so, you'll want to read and memorise every precious detail about your brown-eyed, silky-voiced idol.

NAME: Zayn Javadd Malik
NICKNAMES: 'Zay', 'Z', 'Zaynster'
D.O.B: 12 January 1993
STAR SIGN: Capricorn
FAVE COLOUR: Black
FROM: Bradford, West Yorkshire

ZAYN'S BEST...

ALBUM: Donell Jones
BODY PART: My arms
GRUB: Chicken
FRIEND FOREVER: Liam Payne
STORE: Topman
MOBILE APP: Fat Face
TV SHOW: Family Guy
WAY TO CHILLAX: Having a long lie-in
NIGHT OUT: Going to the cinema
BAND: NSync

CLEVER CLOGS
Music isn't the only area in which Zayn excels. He's a talented artist and a voracious reader who aged just 8 had the reading age of the average 18-year-old. He even sat his English GCSE a year early, landing himself an A!

SCHOOL DAYS
Zayn had a rocky start to his school life because at the first two schools he attended he was the only mixed heritage kid in class. However, aged 12 he and his elder sister moved again to a school with a more cosmopolitan intake where he finally felt at home.

EARLY PROMISE
Zayn was really into drama at school, appearing in musicals like *Arabian Nights* and *Grease*. He even played the lead part in *Bugsy Malone*.

GIRLS, GIRLS, GIRLS
Zayn had his first kiss aged 9, but he was so short he had to stand on a brick! He says he's looking for "someone I feel comfortable around and can spoil a bit". He's recently been spotted out with Little Mix vocalist Perrie Edwards. Zayn's celeb crush is Megan Fox.

FAMILY MAN
Zayn's grandfather was from Pakistan and his maternal grandfather was Irish so he is Irish/English/Asian. He also comes from a really big family. As well as having four sisters, Zayn has five aunties and two uncles on his dad's side alone, plus a clan of over 20 first cousins!

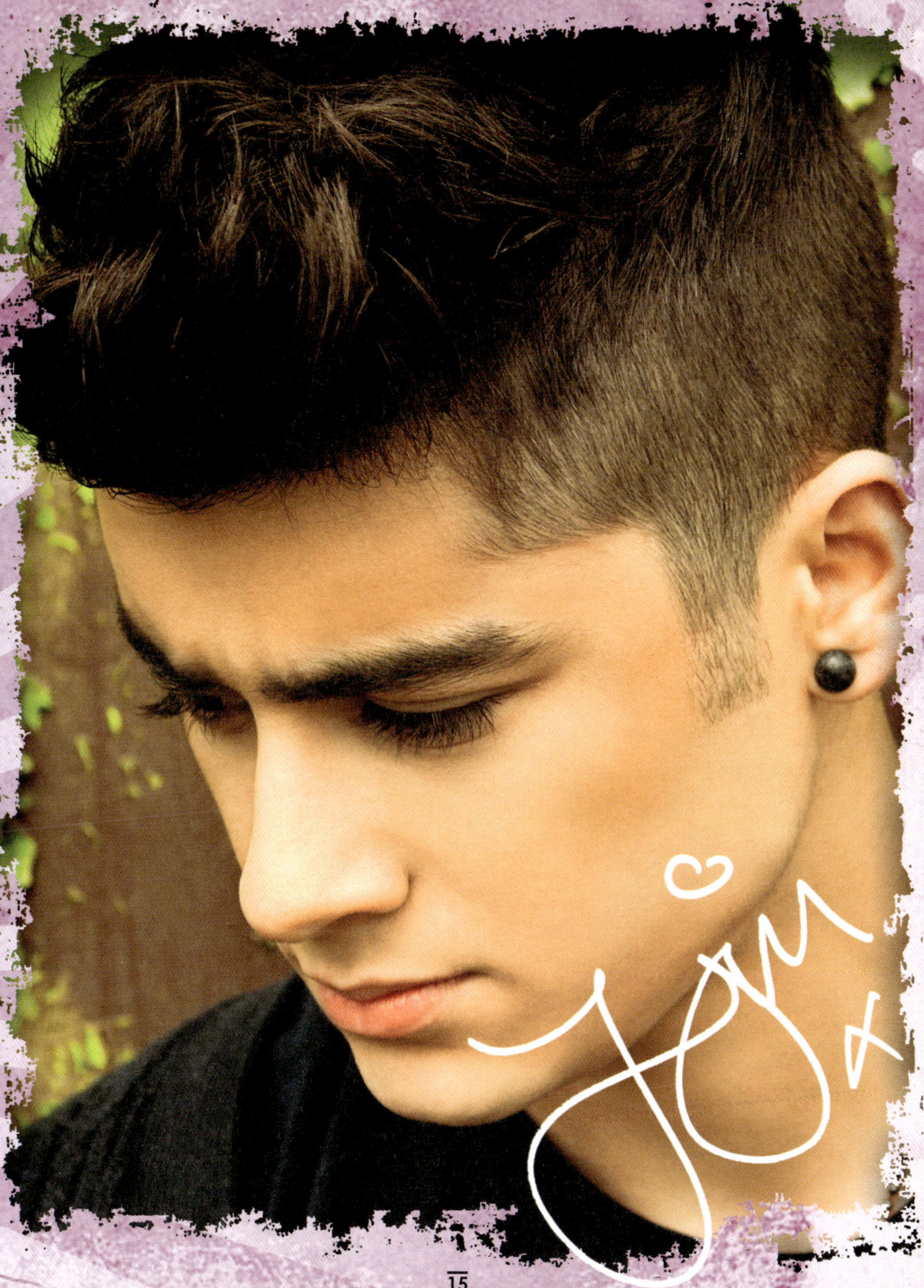

LOVIN' LOUIS

Aaah Louis! He's the green-eyed guy with the cut glass cheekbones and chiseled jaw-line. Let's get to grips with the dude from 'Donny'.

NAME: Louis William Tomlinson
NICKNAMES: 'Luigi', 'Lou', 'Tommo'
D.O.B: 24 December 1991
STAR SIGN: Capricorn
FAVE COLOUR: Red
FROM: Doncaster, South Yorkshire

LOUIS'S BEST...

ALBUM: 'How To Save A Life' by The Fray
BODY PART: My mouth – without it I wouldn't have a job
GRUB: Pasta and pizza
FRIEND FOREVER: Stan
STORE: Topman
MOBILE APP: Twitter
TV SHOW: One Tree Hill and Skins
WAY TO CHILLAX: Breakfast in bed then playing computer games
NIGHT OUT: A great house party
BAND: The Fray

WHAT'S IN A NAME?
Louis was initially named Louis Troy Austin, but his parents split when he was very young and he took his stepfather's surname.

SCHOOL DAYS
Louis was cheeky and chatty at school, but he suffered from moving around a lot and in his teens was rather a party animal. He switched secondary schools twice and failed the first year of A-levels, so had to start again at another school.

EARLY PROMISE
Liam appeared in lots of school productions and did extra work on TV. He met his now good friend James Corden on the set of the show *Fat Friends* and went on to have a part in *Waterloo Road*. Before auditioning for *The X Factor* he was in a band called The Rogue.

GIRLS, GIRLS, GIRLS
Louis goes for chatty, bubbly girls! He is currently dating a lucky Manchester University student called Eleanor Calder. His celeb crush is Cheryl Cole.

WORK ETHIC
Louis has always been a hard-worker. He had many part time jobs while at school - from stacking shelves at Toys R Us to selling popcorn at his local cinema and waiting tables in restaurants. He even had a job selling half-time snacks at Doncaster Rovers' Keepmoat Football Stadium.

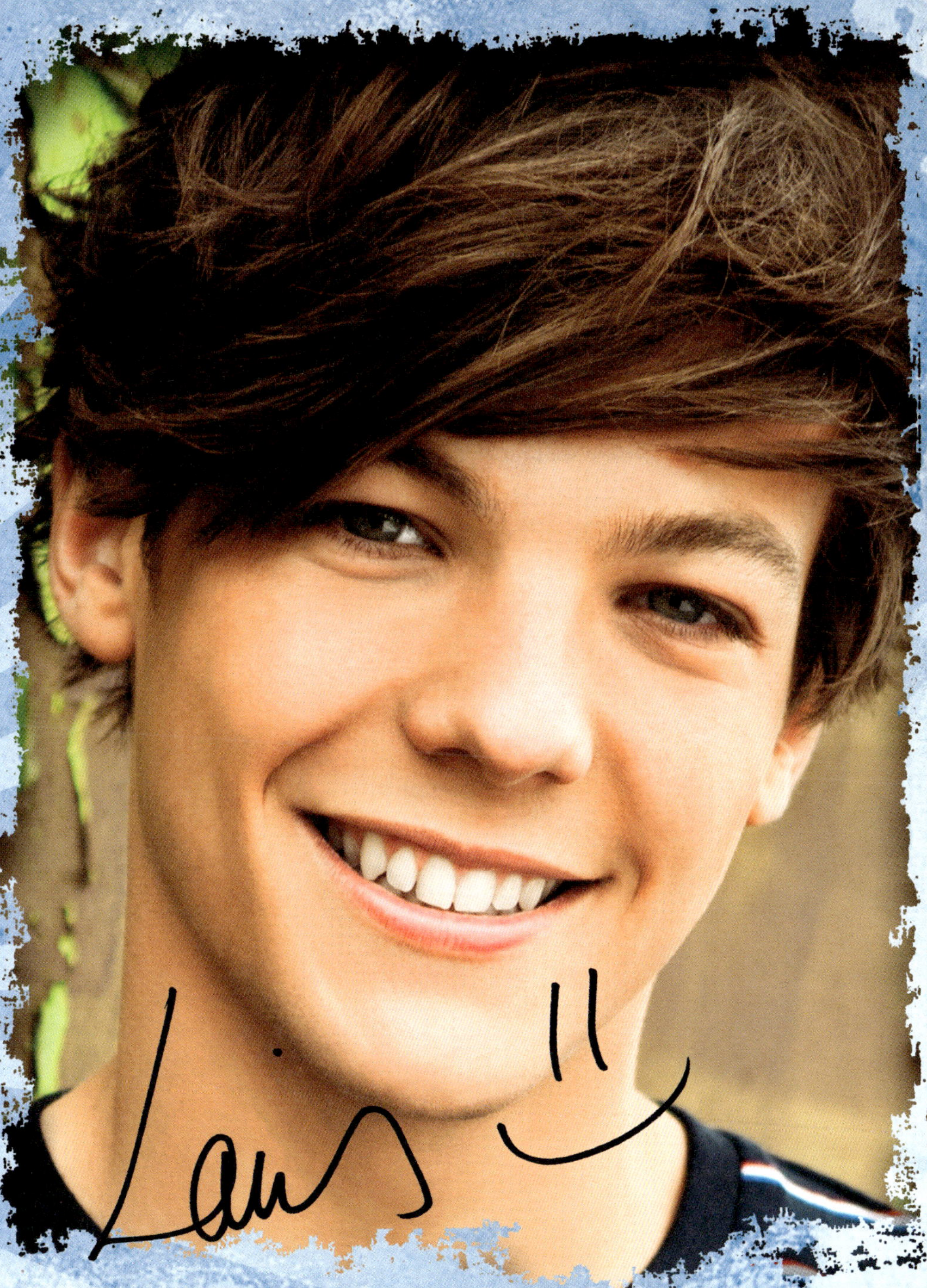

STAR SIGNS

Their success was written in the stars, but what else can the stars tell us about the 1D boys? Answer the five questions below and then see if you can match the zodiac character traits opposite to the correct lad or lads in the band.

2 My star sign is...

3 My star sign is...

1 My star sign is...

A. These kind-hearted guys attract others with their intelligence and humour. They are curious and open-minded and enjoy experiencing new things. They are fiercely independent and don't like to conform, which means they can be very stubborn. When it comes to girls, they like their freedom and tend to shy away from commitment, although when in a relationship they can be very loving.

B. Hard working, determined and tenacious, guys with this star sign always strive hard to have their talents recognized. They value loyalty and have a romantic side, although they can be self-conscious at times. They have excellent fatherly qualities and will eventually want to settle down in a steady relationship with the person they love.

C. Boys with this star sign make great friends. They are so truthful and logical, they are great to come to if you have a problem. Organised, and with perfectionist tendencies, lads with this star sign are more intellectual than flirty and romantic. These guys usually fall for energetic girls who love life, but they don't mind being single and don't need to be in a relationship to feel secure.

4
My star sign is...

5
My star sign is...

WHAT'S IN A NAME?

You scribble their names on your school books, scream them out loud at their concerts and maybe even murmur them in your sleep – but do you know what the 1D boys' monikers really mean? Write each band member's name below its definition.

A

This traditional name has undergone a real revival in recent years, due to a famous book character and its royal connections. It recently overtook Oliver as the most popular boy's name in Britain. Meaning 'home ruler', it sounds very British, but in fact has German origins.

B

This name is shared by a famous rock 'n' roll hellraiser and means 'will' or 'desire'. It is a popular abbreviation of a longer Irish name and is ranked 3rd most popular boys name in the States, while in the UK it currently ranks 39th.

C

This name was very common amongst the French nobility and was borne by 16 French kings, but it still ranks in the top 100 most popular boys names in Britain. More recent famous bearers include a jazz musician, an inventor and a bespectacled British broadcaster.

D

This moniker's exact origins are unclear although it is definitely gaelic. It also has several meanings. It can mean 'champion' but also 'cloud' or 'passionate'. Historically it was the name of someone who founded a dynasty of kings.

E

A famous radio DJ and new music pioneer shares the western version of this exotic first name which has varied spellings. It is Islamic in origin and means 'beauty' or 'handsome'.

TWISTED LYRICS

Can you unscramble the lyrics to these top 1D hits and re-write them in the spaces provided? Once you've done this, write the song title in at the top of each verse.

1

Song title

Nobody you my up world like baby else light

....

2

Song title

Out head out get so out my get get of

....

3

Song title

Know you and oh away fade I walk I'll if

....

4

Song title

Is else 'cause there nobody

....

....

22

5
Song title

What is don't I it don't don't I know

....

6
Song title

Arms instead my and into fall

....

7
Song title

Gets way flip that you your overwhelmed the hair me

....

8
Song title

One but need one that and thing got I you've thing that

....

9
Song title

At it tell ground the to smile when hard but ain't you

....

10
Song title

Know oh don't beautiful you you oh don't you're know

....

TWEET, TWEET

Twitter allows the guys to connect with Directioners all over the world. How closely do you follow their tweets?

MATCH MAKER
Write the correct name next to each Twitter factoid...

A Which 1D member was recently voted Ireland's top Tweeter by an Irish radio station? ....

B Who is the most 'followed' member of the group? ....

C Who averages the most daily tweets? ....

D Which band member follows the least number of Twitter users? ....

E Which two band members are the least prolific tweeters, averaging just two posts a day? ....

WHO'S WHO?
Can you match the band member to their Twitter Profile?

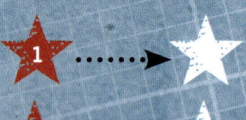

HARRY — 1 → ★

NIALL — 2 → ★

ZAYN — 3 → ★

LOUIS — 4 → ★

LIAM — 5 → ★

A. Hey guys! I'm X from @onedirection; I'm 18 and feeling lucky.

B. It's on like Donkey Kong.

C. Live life for the moment because everything else is uncertain! We would be nowhere without our incredible fans. We owe it all to you.

D. Just close your eyes and enjoy the roller coaster that is life.

E. Hello :) I'm 1/5 of One Direction... And if you follow, thank you... I Love You. Xx

WHICH TWIT SAID IT?
Write the name of the mystery tweeter next to a selection of their Twitter musings...

PERSON A.

1. I either wanna cut my hair short or grow it really long what dya think?

2. Really happy today :D Avocado is my new fave vegetable :)

3. However many amazing things happen in your life you should always be thankful for it, remain humble, modest and respectful :)

PERSON B.

1. Whoops, I ran into Michael Jordan last night! In real life...

2. Just woke up from a dream about being back in maths... really? I dream about THAT???

3. Dropping your sunglasses down the toilet is a mistake you would think that you'd learn from. Apparently not.

PERSON C.

1. Watching the @katyperry movie. Wow, what an amazing woman. True talent!

2. I want to know why @Starbucks don't sell the amazing chicken Santa Fe wraps in the UK. They are incredible.

3. Massive thank you to everyone who has ever supported us. We would be nowhere without you and I assure you we never take it for granted :) xx

PERSON D.

1. Can't wait to go home and watch Jeremy Kyle! #jezzayou'vebeenmissed.

2. Hahahaha! You think my laugh is funny; @ollyofficial has the funniest laugh ever! Sounds like Mutley.

3. Soo cool! Don Henley the lead singer of The Eagles' daughter Annabel came to meet 'n' greet today! My favourite band ever.

PERSON E.

1. I wish I was Iron Man!

2. Well that was embarrassing, just been caught talking to myself and shadow boxing. Lol.

3. So, yesterday you might have heard we went surfing and then fishing and I accidentally caught a tiger shark. Whoops! Will post a picture later.

FACE RACE

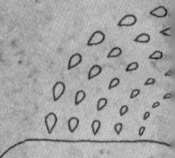

You have 60 seconds to identify and label these facial features. Grab a timer and a pen...

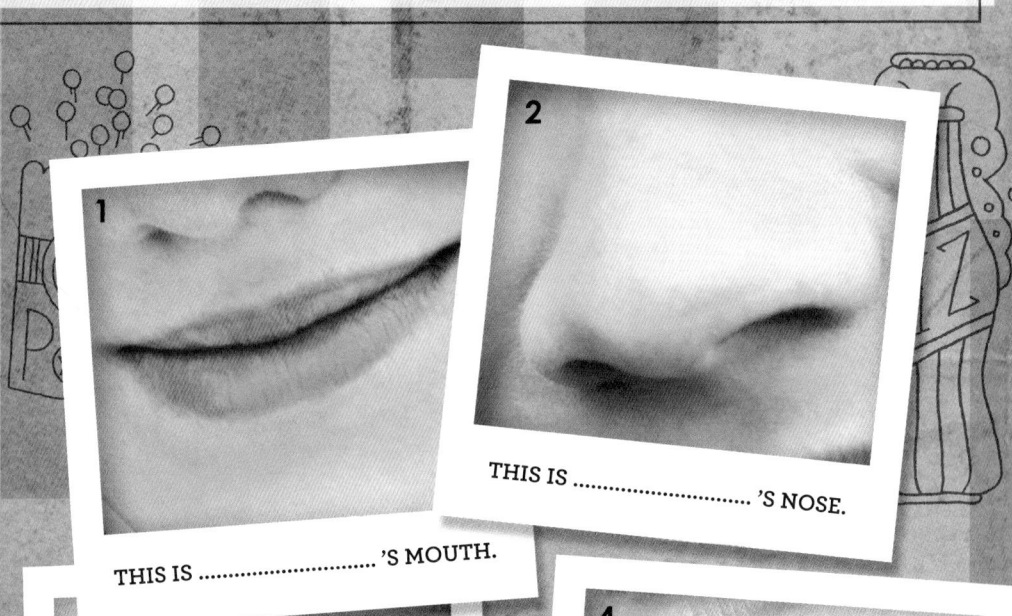

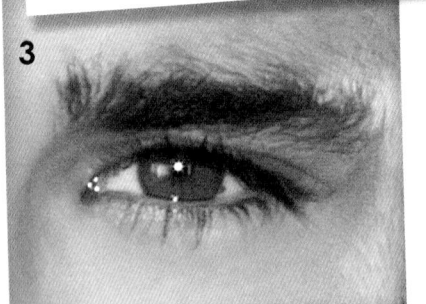

1

THIS IS .... 'S MOUTH.

2

THIS IS .... 'S NOSE.

3

THIS IS .... 'S EYE.

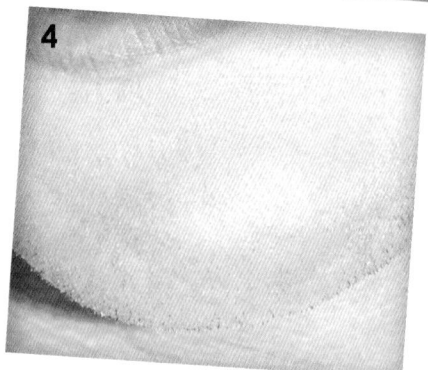

4

THIS IS .... 'S CHIN.

5

THESE ARE .... 'S BROWS.

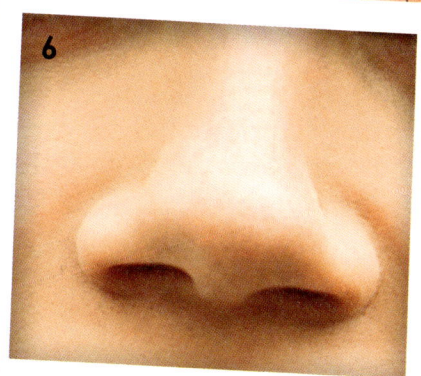

6

THIS IS .... 'S NOSE.

7

THIS IS .... 'S EYE.

8

THIS IS .... 'S EAR.

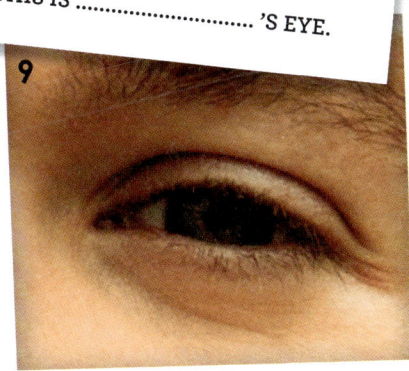

9

THIS IS .... 'S EYE.

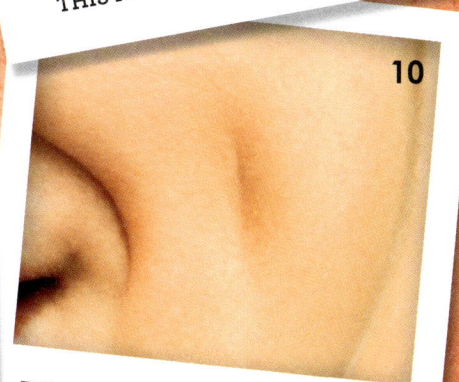

10

THIS IS .... 'S CHEEK.

STAR QUOTES

They're never tongue-tied, the 1D lads. Fill in the blanks in each quote from the list of words along the bottom of the pages and then colour the star next to the quote using the key below.

"When I was little I always said I wanted a .... Now it's like having four of them."

"The .... came out when I had dodgy hair, so I made them take another scan so it looked better."

"I'm a massive ...."

PIGS IN BLANKETS

BARACK OBAMA

DOLL

PAINTBALLING

BOYFRIENDS

MANKINI

"We've been to laser quest and we've said we want to go one further and go .... That's good fun."

"I was starstruck by .... She's an amazing-looking lady, and I'm a massive .... fan anyway."

"I think that .... shouldn't just be limited to Christmas, they should be an all year round kind of thing."

"Louis and I were outside and Louis saw a .... , so he ran up to it and screamed 'Kevin? Is that you?'"

"I have four .... !"

"I like girls who eat .... !"

"Our stylist wants me to do a shoot in a .... I'm up for that."

"Sometimes I see photos and think, 'I do have quite a lot of ....'"

"If you listen to .... album, you'll know that he is one of the best lyricists ever. He knows how to string words together like you wouldn't imagine. We were very lucky to work with him."

MICHELLE OBAMA   **BROTHER**   **HAIR**

ED SHEERAN'S   **SOFTY**   **PIGEON**

CARROTS

ALRIGHT, PET?

Who ever heard of a quiz where the questions already have answers? You have now. Trouble is, the answers are all wrong! Swap them around so that each one connects with the right question.

Who has a dog called Boris and two cats named Rolo and Tom?	1	LOUIS
Who has a hamster called Eleanor, a rabbit called Daisy and a dog called Ted?	2	HARRY
Who has a cat called Dusty?	3	NIALL
Who has two turtles called Boris and Archimedes?	4	ZAYN
Who has a cat called Jess?	5	LIAM

QUICK CRITTER QUIZ

They've had some crazy animal encounters over the years. Test your knowledge about 1D and their furry, feathered and four-legged friends.

1. Who has a fear of birds flying inside?
2. Which huggable animals did Liam and Harry handle while in Australia?
3. Who once said their pet hate was "rabbits – they don't do anything"?
4. Who came up with a cheeky name for Louis' smallest family pet and why?
5. Who recently said they would like a pet chimpanzee?
6. What happened when Liam left his pets in the care of his girlfriend while on tour?
7. Whose first pet was a Staffordshire bull terrier dog called Tyson?
8. Who was attacked by a goat as a child?

1. ....
2. ....
3. ....
4. ....
5. ....
6. ....
7. ....
8. ....

CRUSHWORD

Solve the clues and fill in the blanks to find the names of the lucky ladies the 1D lads just lurve....

ACROSS

4. Mr Tomlinson's real-life, student girlfriend. [7, 6]
5. Little Mix vocalist, who steps out with Zayn. [6,7]
6. Sexy The Saturdays member, who sets Harry's pulse racing. [7,8]
7. *The X Factor* contestant turned West End star, admired by Louis. [5,7]
8. Niall fancies this 'Promise This' and 'Call My Name' songstress. [5,4]

DOWN

1. Zayn gets hot under the collar over this *Transformers* actress. [5,3]
2. Liam's long-term, dancer girlfriend. [8,6]
3. _____ Lewis, female singer adored by Liam. [5]

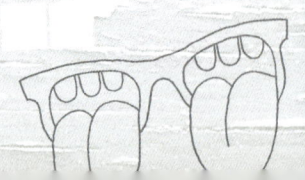

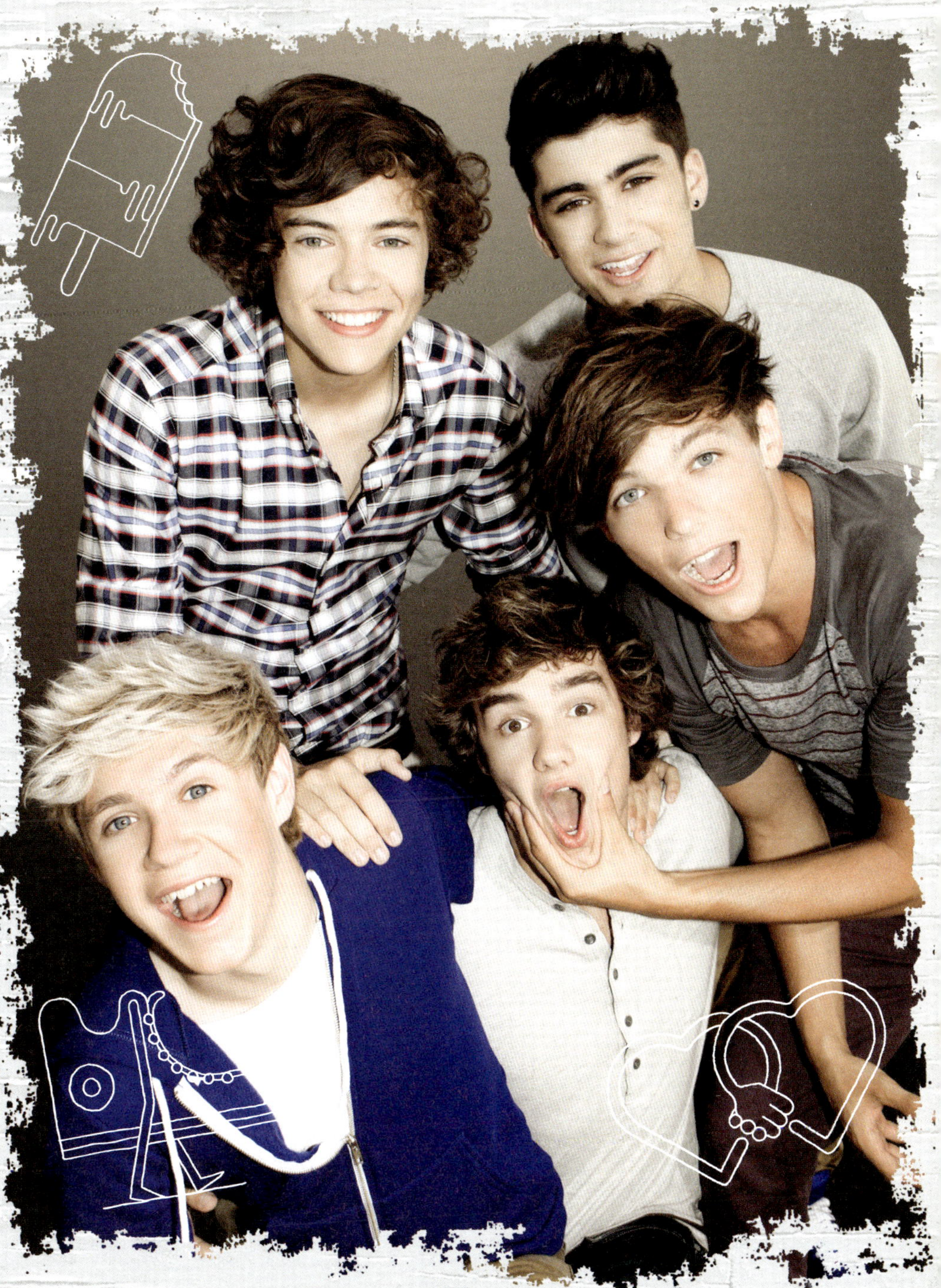

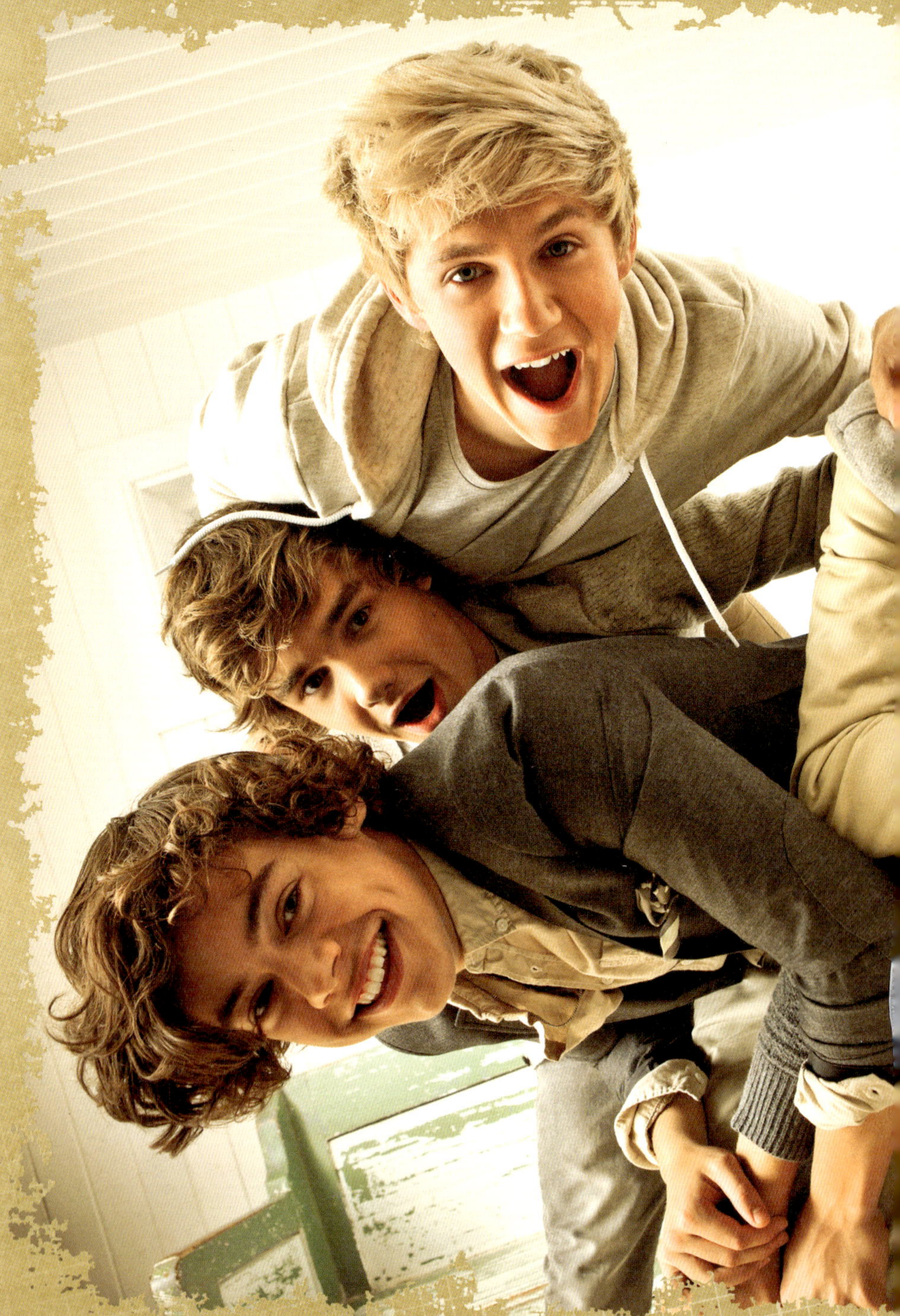

35

YOU'RE THE BEST

Which of these awards are currently gracing the boys' mantelpieces? Grab a pen and colour in the trophy icon next to the awards the group have already scooped.

1. UK Nickleodeon Kid's Choice Awards 2012 – Favourite UK Band

2. Glamour Awards 2012 – Best Band

3. Teen Choice Awards 2012 – Best Love Song

4. Rear of the Year 2011 – Harry Styles

5. TRL Awards 2012 – Best Fans

6. UK Nickleodeon Kid's Choice Awards 2012 – Favourite UK Newcomer

7. Grammy Awards 2012 – Best International group

BRIT Awards 2012
– Best Single 'What Makes You Beautiful'

4Music Video Honours 2011
– Best Group

Teen Choice Awards 2012
– Breakout Group

Blue Peter Book Awards 2012
– Best Children's Book 'Dare to Dream'

Logie Awards 2012
– Most Popular New Male Talent

WHO WORE IT?

They could dress in bin-bags and still look cool. Draw a line between each (sometimes crazy) piece of clothing and the gorgeous guy who sported it.

FUNNY TEE

COMIC CLOTHING

BRACE YOURSELF

LOVELY LAPELS

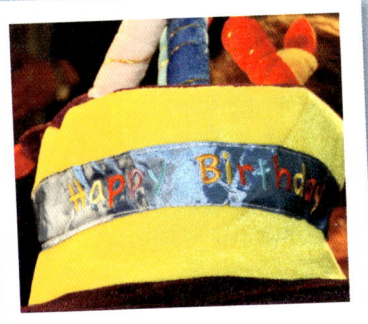

MANY HATTY RETURNS

70'S VIBE

DICKIE BOW

GRANNY KNIT

BASEBALL JACKET

ONESIES RULE

1-D WARDROBE

Which of these looks are firmly ensconsed in the One Direction wardrobe and which would never make the cut? Copy the bona fide 1D trends into the wardrobe opposite.

PREPPY AMERICAN BASEBALL JACKETS
SLOGAN TEES
MAN BAGS
TIED HOODIES
PATTERNED TIGHTS (FOR MEN)
CONTRASTING BRACES
CHECKED SHIRTS
HUNTER WELLIES WITH BOARD SHORTS
NAUTICAL STRIPES AND BLAZERS
HEAD TO TOE DENIM
SMART TAILORING
BOW TIES
KILTS

SHOE WHO?

Which two 1D-ers are being described here?

.... can never have too many pairs of Toms Shoes.

.... is a huge fan of Supra trainers.

UP ALL NIGHT

The 1D boys were up all night every night, during their aptly named 'Up All Night' tour. Unjumble the anagrams below to reveal the names of some of the hottest venues and biggest destinations that the lads played.

VENUES OF THE WORLD

1. HET 2O — DUBLIN
2. MONITORTOP NEARA — CARDIFF
3. MVH MATHSHIMMER LOPALO — LONDON
4. NATIONAL RODONI NEARA — BIRMINGHAM
5. CHOE NEARA — LIVERPOOL

1. ....
2. ....
3. ....
4. ....
5. ....

DREAM DESTINATIONS

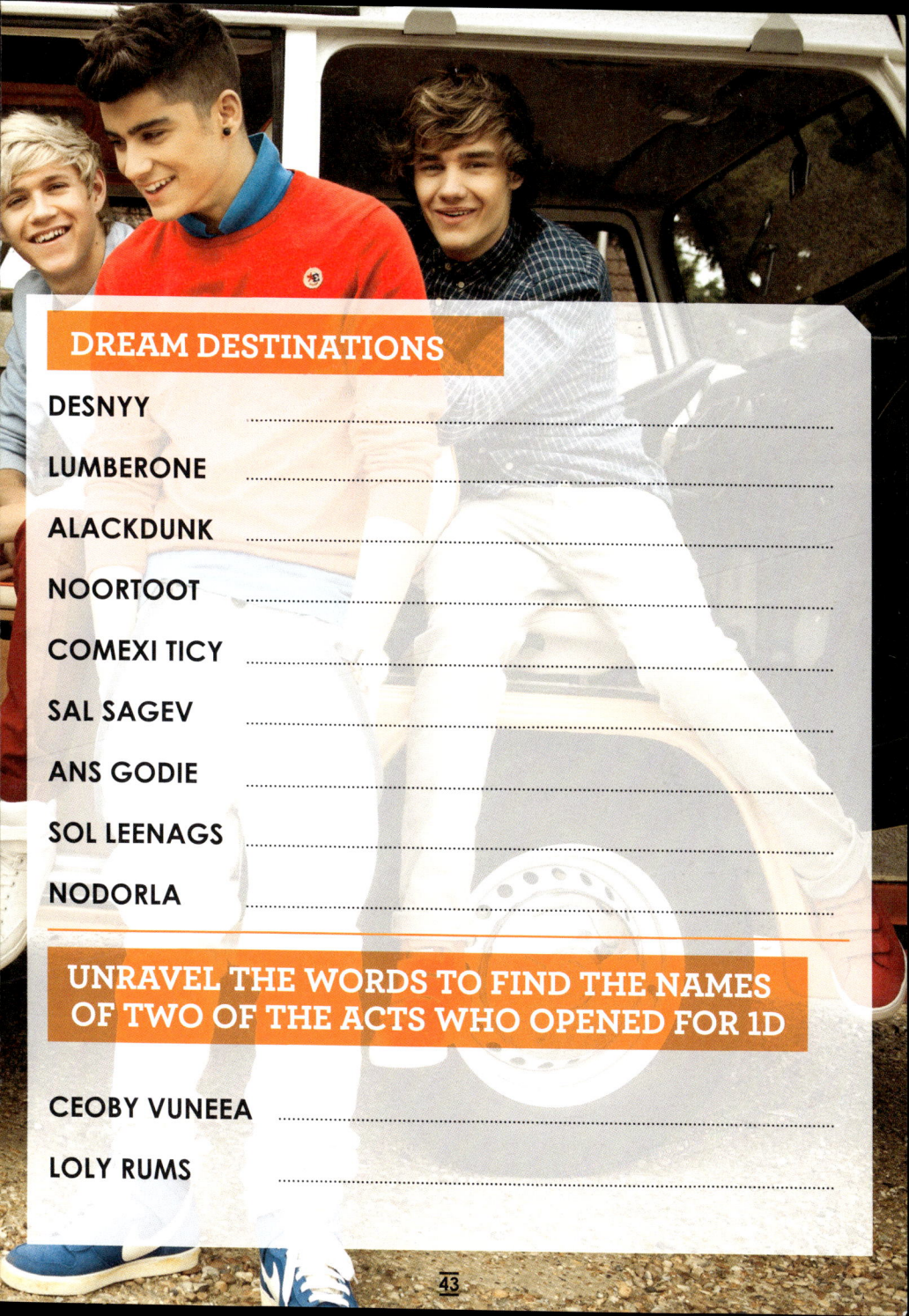

DESNYY ....

LUMBERONE ....

ALACKDUNK ....

NOORTOOT ....

COMEXI TICY ....

SAL SAGEV ....

ANS GODIE ....

SOL LEENAGS ....

NODORLA ....

UNRAVEL THE WORDS TO FIND THE NAMES OF TWO OF THE ACTS WHO OPENED FOR 1D

CEOBY VUNEEA ....

LOLY RUMS ....

WHAT GOES ON TOUR...

... does not always stay on tour. Which of the following events really occurred while the boys were on the road?

1 Louis Tomlinson wore reindeer slippers while relaxing in the dressing room or on the tour bus.
● SURE DID   ● NAH, NEVER

2 Niall voluntarily shaved his own nipples.
● SURE DID
● NAH, NEVER

3 1D's security found a stinky fan hiding in a bin backstage
● SURE DID
● NAH, NEVER

4 Zayn got a tattoo of a microphone on his arm.
● SURE DID   ● NAH, NEVER

5 Niall hurt his thumb during a Nerf gun battle onstage.
● SURE DID
● NAH, NEVER

6 Harry ran about backstage in his boxers before pretending to shave his legs with a razor.
● SURE DID
● NAH, NEVER

44

7 Three lads suffered whiplash when a car hit the tour bus.
○ SURE DID
○ NAH, NEVER

8 Niall met the Obamas and fainted.
○ SURE DID ○ NAH, NEVER

9 Liam caught a shark on a fishing trip.
○ SURE DID
○ NAH, NEVER

10 Harry accidentally dyed Niall's hair red.
○ SURE DID
○ NAH, NEVER

11 A male guest tried to get into Louis Tomlinson's hotel room when he got lost after a night out.
○ SURE DID ○ NAH, NEVER

12 Louis stepped on Niall's hairbrush and ended up on crutches.
○ SURE DID
○ NAH, NEVER

13 Harry challenged Justin Bieber to a duel over Selena Gomez.
○ SURE DID ○ NAH, NEVER

14 Louis bungee jumped off Auckland Sky Tower, clad in a fetching blue and yellow lycra suit.
○ SURE DID
○ NAH, NEVER

BUBBLE BANTER

What do the lads really think of one another? Decide who is talking then write their quote into the correct speech bubble.

QUOTES...

"Niall's a bit crazy. He's so much fun and he never stops. It must be exhausting being him."

"On the plane, Harry got up and went to the toilet in just a blanket – who does that?"

"My first real crush was Louis Tomlinson."

"Zayn and me are Captain Zappers, the others are in the club, but they're not captains."

"At bootcamp Liam was quite different, quiet, very sensible, kept to himself, but after a while he blossomed into this fine young man."

WORDSEARCH

You'll need to keep 'em peeled if you're going to find all the 1-D names hiding in the grid opposite...

Z	Q	M	K	G	R	W	E	N	Y	A	P
T	H	A	R	R	Y	N	L	X	Y	I	P
W	H	O	A	K	J	U	F	R	E	D	U
X	V	R	I	T	T	S	I	U	O	L	X
L	N	L	H	O	R	A	N	X	U	I	A
X	A	S	I	M	T	V	J	N	F	A	C
M	H	G	N	L	E	D	O	W	U	M	L
Q	K	H	P	I	Y	M	D	P	B	X	L
N	O	D	W	N	I	Q	U	M	R	E	E
S	Y	V	X	S	T	Y	L	E	S	V	W
K	Y	A	M	O	T	N	S	W	M	T	O
E	T	X	Z	N	A	I	L	L	G	I	C

HARRY   **LIAM**   **MALIK**   **PAYNE**   **TOMLINSON**
HORAN   **LOUIS**   **NIALL**   **STYLES**   **ZAYN**

THINK YOU'RE DONE...

Nuh Uh! There are two more names to find. You're looking for the christian and surnames of an influential person who is very important to the 1D boys.

__ __ __ __ __   __ __ __ __ __ __ __

MIX PICS

Can you work out which pair of band members are jumbled up in each of these two pictures? Write your answers below.

A

Can you guess?

B

Can you guess?

Use this space to write down all the reasons why these boys are unique and why you'd never, ever get them muddled up in real life.

DREAM DAYS

Imagine your ultimate 24 hours with 1D. How would you spend your time? Which magical memories would you create? Simply tick your perfect preferences!

Spend the day at a waterpark with Niall ☐
OR
watch a footie match with him? ☐

Walk your dogs with Louis ☐
OR
have him as your personal stylist on a shopping spree? ☐

Have a sleepover at Harry's house ☐
OR
take him to your school prom? ☐

Spend the day writing songs with Liam ☐
OR
be his training partner at the gym for the day? ☐

Let Zayn cook you a private dinner ☐
OR
go ice-skating with him? ☐

Get a massage next to Liam ☐
OR
go surfing with him? ☐

Go 'Toms' shopping with Louis ☐
OR
have an all-day computer game-a-thon with him? ☐

Have Zayn show you round his home town ☐
OR
perform a duet with him in front of your friends? ☐

Have a dance-off on the Wii with Harry ☐
OR
go to the movies to watch a rom-com with him? ☐

Be Niall's personal assistant for the day ☐
OR
make a video diary with him? ☐

Spend the day backstage with the boys ☐
OR
have the boys hang with you in your 'hood for the day? ☐

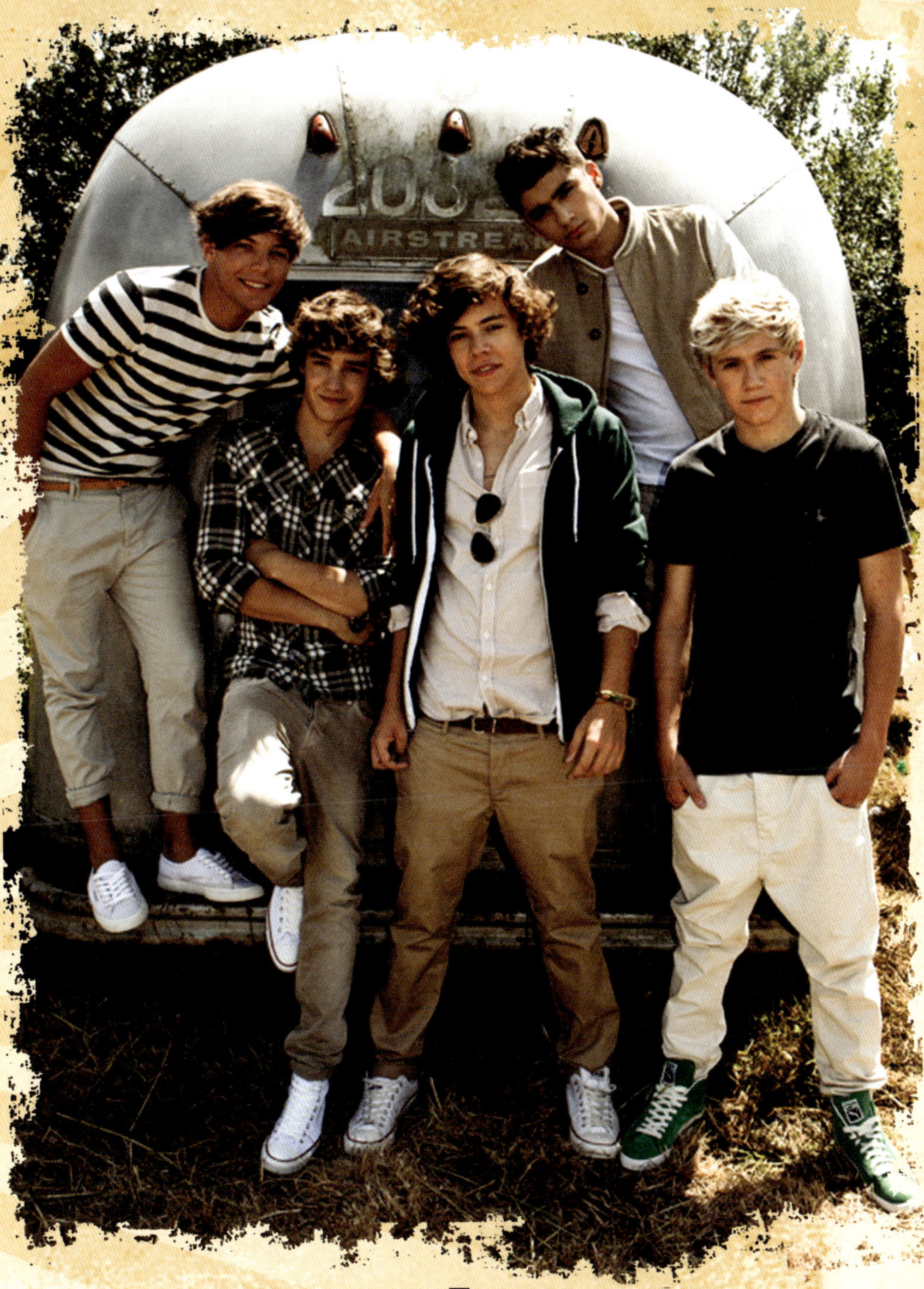
AIRSTREAM

VA VA VIDEO

The group love shooting the music videos to accompany their songs. Read the statements below and decide which video each one is referring to.

Answer 1:
This vid was filmed in Malibu.

Answer 2:
The boys camped by a wooded lake with a bonfire.

The lads jumped down a hill on space hoppers.
Answer 3:

Answer 4:
The group were on a stage made to look like a wood-panelled school room.

Answer 5: The boys frolicked in the waves.

Answer 6: Louis zipped around in a blue mini, while Zayn took the train.

Answer 7: Zayn embraced a girl at sunset.

Answer 8: The lads jumped on a red leather Chesterfield sofa.

Answer 9: This vid was shot in Lake Placid, New York.

Answer 10: Louis got pulled over for driving an orange camper van too slowly during this shoot.

Answer 11: This clip was filmed in London and showed the lads performing to fans in Covent Garden.

Answer 12: Girls in the audience screamed and sang along to this song.

PRANK-STARS

They look like butter wouldn't melt, but boys will be boys. 1D just love to pull pranks on each other and even their fans, too. Are you au fait with their latest hi-jinks?

1. Whose hand did Louis dunk in water in an attempt to make him wee while sleeping?

2. Harry recently shared one of Louis's fave pranks saying "I'm always waking up to find ………………… shoved up my nose." Which item does Louis put up Harry's nose?

3. During *The X Factor* tour Louis jumped on Harry's back and the pair ran round someone while they were trying to sing – who?

4. Who complained that Louis "regularly breaks into my room and throws buckets of water over me when I'm sleeping"?

5. Which band member got pranked when the others arranged to rap 'The Fresh Prince of Bel Air' without him knowing anything about it?

6. Which hair-related stunt did Niall pull recently, posting the pictures of himself on his Twitter page?

7. During a photo-shoot for *The X Factor*, what did Liam dare Louis to do to Simon Cowell?

8. Which band member had his mouth taped up by the other lads during a video diary, in an attempt to keep him quiet?

9. When, on April Fool's Day Louis tweeted he was going to be a dad, who did they announce was pregnant with his child?

10. Which baby-related prank did two of the lads play on the others on live TV?

SPOT THE DIFFERENCE

Phwoar! This pic of the guys is so totes gorge we printed it twice! BTW there are six subtle differences to spot...

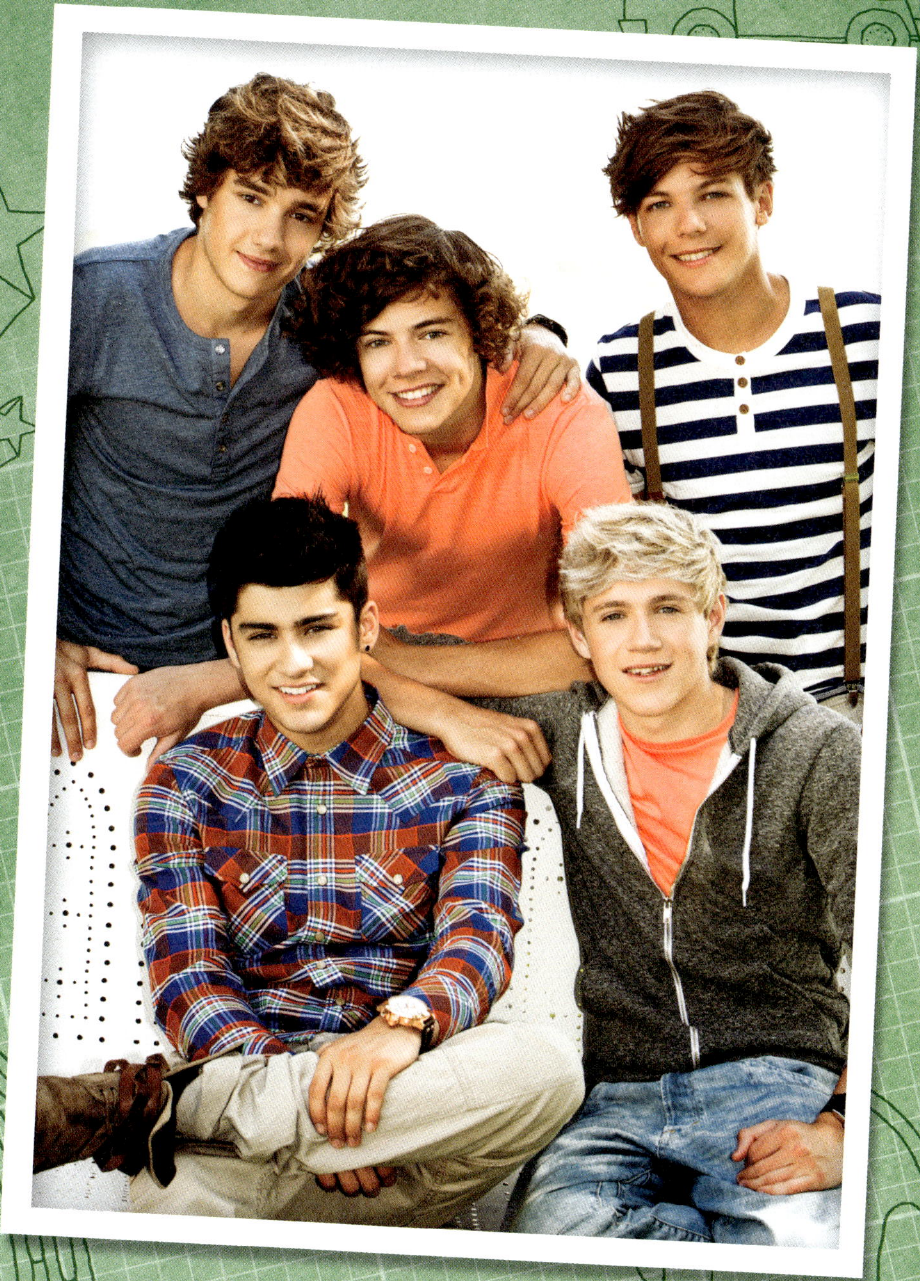

HARRY: QUICK QUIZ

Grab a pen and see how quickly you can answer these questions about Hazza. Circle the T if you think the statement is true or the F if you think it's false.

1 When Harry was younger he had straight hair. — T/F

2 Harry is the eldest member of 1D. — T/F

3 Harry's audition song was 'Don't Leave me This Way' by The Communards. — T/F

4 Harry does not like mayonnaise. — T/F

| 5 | *Love Actually* is one of Harry's favourite films. | T/F |

| 6 | Harry is from Yorkshire. | T/F |

| 7 | Harry has a five-pointed star tattoo – a point for every member of 1D. | T/F |

| 8 | Harry suffers from arachnophobia – the fear of spiders. | T/F |

MISSING LYRICS

Four song titles and lots of missing words are floating around on these pages. Can you choose the right word to put into each slot to complete four famous 1D tracks?

....
We've got a bit of love ....
You take me to the edge then you hit the ....
I .... it's over one day.
But then I'm .... back, begging
you to ....

TAKEN   **MORE THAN THIS**   **HAVE**   **BLINDED**
FOREVER YOUNG   **NA NA NA**   **SLEPT**   **HEART**

....
I'm ....,
Do you .... me?
I'm ....,
Cause you are .... I see.
I'm ...., alone.
I'm praying,
That your .... will just .... around.

62

EVERYTHING BROKEN EXPECTING
CRAWLING SAY BOMB MOVED ON
WAIT WATCHING TURN BRAKES ONE

....

Let's .... in style.
Let's dance for a ....
Heaven can .... , we're only .... the skies.
Hoping for the best but .... the worst.
Are you gonna .... the .... or not?

....

Now that you can't .... me, you .... want me. Now that I'm with .... else you tell me you .... me.
I .... on your doorstep, begging for .... chance.
Now that I finally ...., you say that you .... me all ....

MISSED SOMEBODY WANT ALONG
DANCING HATE SUDDENLY DROP
STAY HEAR DANCE WHILE

ON THE COVER

The boys love to put their unique stamp on fantastic songs. Can you match their favourite cover versions with the artist who previously sang them?

- STEREO HEARTS
- VALERIE
- TORN
- USE SOMEBODY
- I GOTTA FEELING

- NATALIE IMBRUGLIA
- KINGS OF LEON
- BLACK EYED PEAS
- THE ZUTONS
- GYM CLASS HEROES

They've graced the covers of magazines around the world. These U.K. and U.S. mags have all featured the guys on their front page – except one. Can you guess which and cross it out?

J-14

FABULOUS

WE LOVE POP

BILLBOARD MAGAZINE

PEOPLE MAGAZINE

SUGAR

TEEN NOW

GRAZIA

TOP OF THE POPS

ROLLING STONE

LOUIS: QUICK QUIZ

You should really be getting to know Louis by now. Grab a pen and get answering! Circle the T if you think the statement is true and around the F if you think it's false.

1 — Louis is 6ft tall. — T/F

2 — He is the most untidy member of the band. — T/F

3 — His middle name is William. — T/F

4 — He once 'mooned' his headmaster. — T/F

| 5 | He speaks fluent Italian. | T/F |

| 6 | He has four sisters. | T/F |

| 7 | He has a tattoo of a microphone on his arm. | T/F |

| 8 | His birthday is on New Year's Eve. | T/F |

LOOK LIVELY!

Take a long, hard look at the photo. Set a timer for 60 seconds. When your time's up, cover the picture and see how many of the questions you can answer correctly.

Remember no sneak re-peeks and when you're done, the answers are on page 95.

1. What is Harry doing with his hands in the picture?

2. Who is in the centre of the shot?

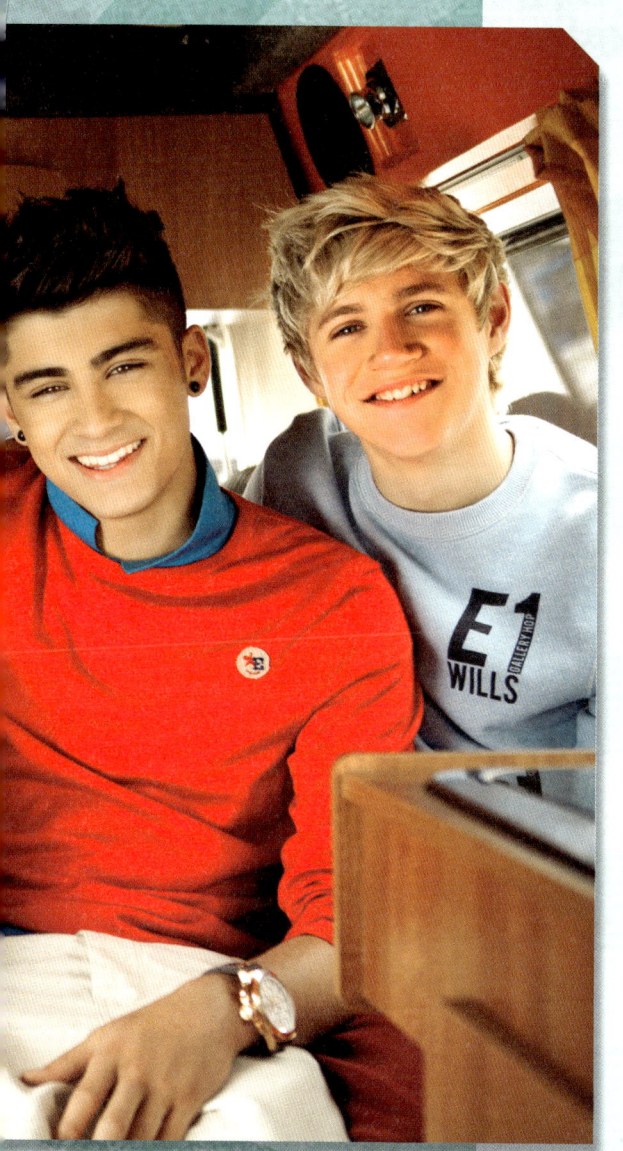

3. How many members are wearing red items of clothing?

4. Is Liam's top button done up or not?

5. How many watches are visible?

6. Which capital letter and which number appear in the logo on Niall's sweatshirt

7. What pattern is on the hankie in Harry's jacket pocket?

8. Is Liam leaning towards Harry or Zayn?

9. Where do you think the boys are being photographed?

10. What colours and pattern are the curtains at the windows?

PHONE A FRIEND

Here's a fun way to liven up your day. Why not get your BFF on the phone and bond over your mutual love of the boys with this 1D Spelling Bee.

All you have to do is to set your timer and see how quickly he or she can answer these 1D-related spelling questions. Give her a tick or a cross in the box next to the answer we've provided, and then tot up her score and ring the statement which best applies to her fan status.

1. Spell Louis's surname.
TOMLINSON

2. Spell the last word in the title of their first hit single.
BEAUTIFUL

3. Spell the country in which Niall was born.
IRELAND

4. Spell the name of Zayn's home city.
BRADFORD

5. Spell the surname of Cher, who came fourth in the same *The X Factor* series the boys starred in.
LLOYD

6 Spell former *The X Factor* judge Dani's surname.
MINOGUE

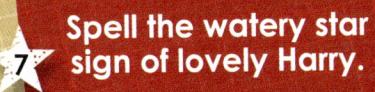

7 Spell the watery star sign of lovely Harry.
AQUARIUS

8 Spell 'unbelievable success' – 1D certainly enjoy this…
UNBELIEVABLE SUCCESS

Your BFF's score was ……………….. out of 8. She's….

A TRUE DIRECTIONER ☐

ON THE RIGHT PATH TO DIRECTIONISM ☐

TOTALLY LOST AND NEEDS RE-DIRECTION ☐

ZAYN: QUICK QUIZ

How fast can you answer these questions about Zayn? Just draw a circle around the T if you think the statement is true and around the F if you think it's false.

1 — The original spelling of Zayn's name was Zain – but he prefers it with a 'y'. — **T/F**

2 — His paternal grandfather is from Iran. — **T/F**

3 — Zayn can't swim. — **T/F**

4 — He held Harry's hand when Harry got his first tattoo. — **T/F**

| 5 | He didn't have a passport before he was on *The X Factor*. | T/F |

| 6 | His favourite aftershave is *One Million* by Paco Rabanne. | T/F |

| 7 | He loves to draw. | T/F |

| 8 | He was in a band called White Eskimo at school. | T/F |

STARRY QUOTES

We all love the 1D boys, but what do their fellow celebs think of them? Can you match each starry quote with the famous person who said it?

a "We never worked on anything, we just hung out, they're just cool."

b "We met them two years ago when they were on *The X Factor* – they're all really nice lads and we met them again in Los Angeles. They're bigger than us – they've got more money than me."

c "We're going to be touring with them. They're awesome guys, we just met them the day before we flew out here. And our fans, if they don't already know them, they're excited to get to know them."

1. Olly Murs 2. Tom Parker *The Wanted* 3. Joe Jonas 4. Simon Cowell

ANSWERS: 1. ★ + ○   2. ★ + ○   3. ★ + ○

d "They sang their song 'What Makes You Beautiful'. It was all of our first times meeting these guys and they were really nice… They did a good job."

f "They are what they are, you know? They are just five young guys having a great time. That's what I love about them. What you see is what you get."

e "I'm pretty excited to go over to do this BBC1 Radio Show that's coming up, with my good friend Pixie Lott and this group One Direction that people are loving right now. They're super talented and they seem like cool dudes so it should be a really fun show."

g "They've worked hard. They work really well as a group. The records are good. They're nice guys to work with. So the world, right now, is theirs."

5. James Maslow
Big Time Rush

6. Justin Bieber

7. Miranda Cosgrove
iCarly

4. ★ + ○   5. ★ + ○   6. ★ + ○   7. ★ + ○

PET PUZZLER

Can you work out which of the boys' pets are being described in these fun rhymes? When you're done, write the name of each pet's owner in the space provided.

A

I'm a singer's best friend,
And I love a long walk.
I'll give you a bark,
And it's like I can talk.
When you come home to stay,
I'll lay down on your bed.
I live with the family,
And my name is ....

... and I belong to ....

B

I come from oop north,
And I'm soft to the touch.
I've thousands of followers,
On Facebook and such.
Creatures like me are inherently cool,
Though we really can't stand to hang out by the pool.
The studs on our collars might just get rusty,
And our species hate water, yes my name is………………………………

… and I belong to…………………………

LIAM: QUICK QUIZ

It's time for a quick fire round on the lovely Liam. Just draw a circle around the T if you think the statement is true and around the F if you think it's false.

1 Liam only has one functioning lung. — T/F

2 He usually wears Calvin Klein underwear. — T/F

3 He used to be a boy scout. — T/F

4 He has a strange fear of spoons and eats ice-cream with a fork. — T/F

| 5 | His favourite colour is green. | T/F |

| 6 | Before finding fame he was studying catering at college. | T/F |

| 7 | His favourite films are the *Shrek* movies. | T/F |

| 8 | He has two pet turtles. | T/F |

BRAIN TEASER

How many words or phrases can you make from the phrase below? Each word has to be at least three letters long. We've started you off...

ONE DIRECTION

1. Note
2. Ruler
3. Slide
4. ......
5. ......
6. ......
7. ......
8. ......
9. ......
10. ......
11. ......
12. ......

ION RULES

13. ....

14. ....

15. ....

16. ....

17. ....

18. ....

19. ....

20. ....

21. ....

22. ....

23. ....

24. ....

SPORTS DAY

Like all boys 1D play, watch and dream about sport. Can you sprint through the following sports-related quezzies? Or will you trip at the first hurdle?

1 1D celebrated their US number one, with which sports-related treat?

2 With which English magician did Niall recently play pool, during a lad's night in?

3 When the boys visited Las Vegas, what uber-cool sporty feature did their swanky hotel suite boast?

4 The lads recently posted a clip of themselves on Boston Common on VEVO, playing which sport?

5 Which two sports were Liam and Louis pictured trying, while down under in Australia and New Zealand?

6. Which mega star recently invited 1D to join an L.A. celebrity football team he's setting up?

7. Which 1D member is a talented runner who was once on the reserve list for the British squad for the 2012 Olympics?

8. How many members of 1D support Manchester United?

9. Which sporting holiday did Harry and Louis take following the end of *The X Factor* tour?

10. Which famous American basketball player did Harry tweet a picture of himself with?

11. Which wheeled item of sports equipment was Zayn recently pictured holding while in Florida?

12. One Direction flew the flag for Britain by opening the closing ceremony of which major sporting event in 2012?

TREE OF FRIENDS

Circle each leaf containing the name of someone close to 1D and draw a line attaching it to the band member who calls them a friend.

MARTIN

CURTIS

BRAD

SCOTT

SEAN

ANDY

DILLAN

ROB

ANTHONY

JOHN

BEN

DANNY

RONNIE

NICK

AQUIB

STAN

SPOT THE DIFFERENCE

You're supposed to sit in it not on it boys! Can you find six differences between these shots of the lads riding on the back of this cool vintage caravan?

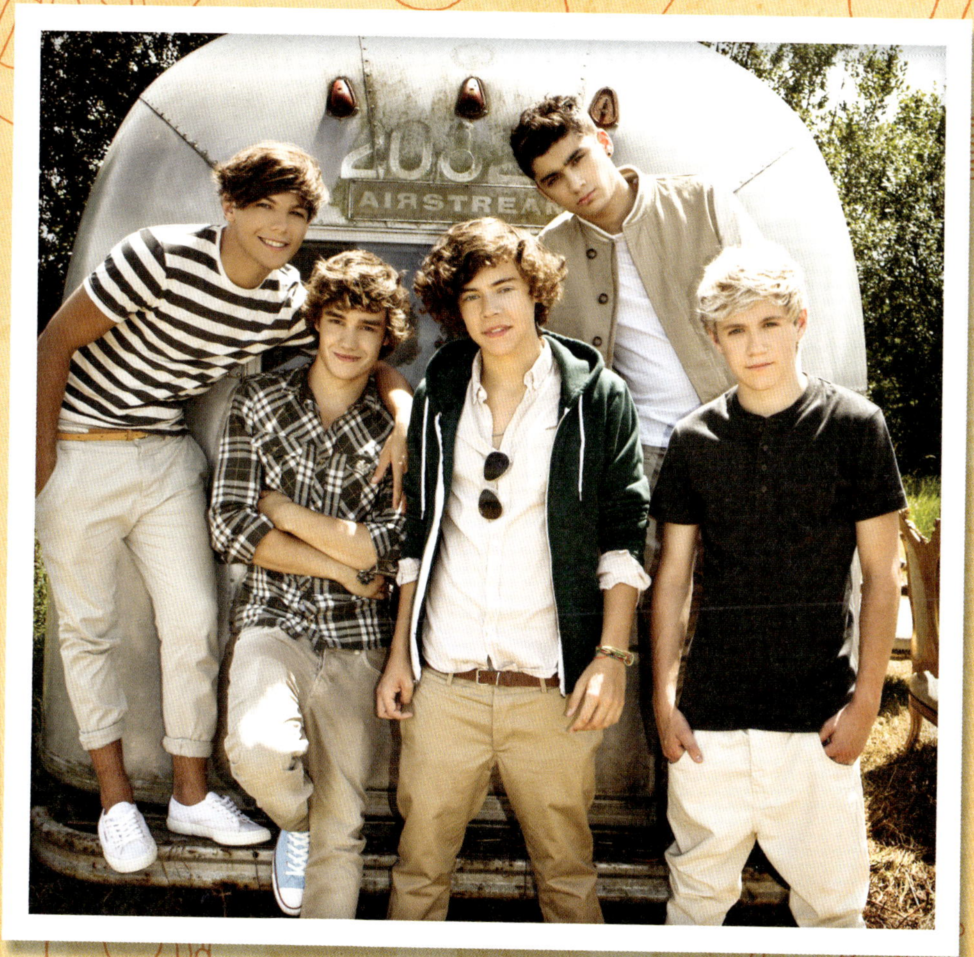

NIALL: QUICK QUIZ

Niall's turn now! You know the drill – just draw a circle around the T if you think the statement is true and around the F if you think it's false.

1 — Niall has a collection of Birkenstock sandals. — T/F

2 — He had to be escorted out of the studio by Liam when he met Justin Bieber – so he could scream in excitement. — T/F

3 — He has a mug featuring a picture of himself on the toilet. — T/F

4 — Niall has never had a job. — T/F

| 5 | He came top in Sugarscape's '50 hottest males of 2011'. | T/F |

| 6 | He speaks excellent Spanish. | T/F |

| 7 | He once sleepwalked and ended up in Louis' bed. | T/F |

| 8 | He hates his own company. | T/F |

KEY CHAINS

Follow the clues down the chain to try and discover which 1D-er is being described.

A

Loves cooking.

Once worked in Toys R Us.

Has a nose like this...

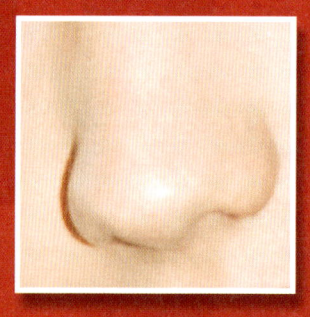

Likes knee high socks on a girl.

Is a Virgo.

Supports West Bromwich Albion.

I AM _____

B

Wears a size 8.5 shoe.

Is afraid of heights.

Was given the contestant serial number 165616 on *The X Factor*.

Has his left ear pierced...

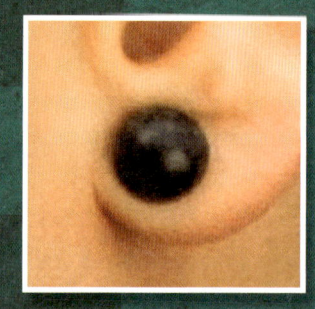

Likes to brush his teeth before going on stage.

Was born in a hospital called St Luke's.

I AM _____

ONE DIRECTION

C

Hates baked beans.

Has a grandmother who competed in the 1936 Olympics at javelin.

Played the part of Danny Zuko in Grease.

Has blue eyes

Had to retake a year in school.

Quite likes chilli flavoured ice-cream.

Once injured his foot on a sea urchin.

I AM _____

THE TRICKY SIX

So, you are a loyal and knowledgeable fan of the boys, but are you their number 1 super fan? Answer the Tricky Six to find out and then turn to page 96 for the answers.

1 Before Harry came up with the name One Direction, the band were originally going to be called something else. What?

....

2 What did Liam once say his super power would be?

....

3 After a performance on ITV show *Dancing On Ice*, which track did Louis say the band would choose to skate to if they were participating?

....

4
After which TV show did Harry cry because he thought he'd ruined the performance?

....

5
Which 1D member is left handed?

....

6
How long did it take 1D to sell out their Madison Square Garden dates?

....

1 – 2 CORRECT

Are you their number 1 fan? 'Na Na Na!' Turn back to the cover and start swotting again! You may be 'Up All Night' but we're sure you can score 'More Than This'!

3 – 4 CORRECT

A good effort! 'Everything About You' screams devoted Directioner. There's just 'One Thing' or two, which tripped you up this time.

5 – 6 CORRECT

Yay! 'Stand Up' and be proud. You truly are a super fan and that's 'What Makes You Beautiful' in the boys' eyes!

ANSWERS

PAGES 2 – 3
Harry Styles

PAGES 4 – 5
Liam sang the Michael Bublé big band version of 'Cry Me a River' by Arthur Hamilton.
Zayn sang 'Let Me Love You' by Mario.
Harry sang 'Isn't She Lovely' by Stevie Wonder.
Niall sang 'So Sick' by Ne-Yo.
Louis sang 'Hey There Delilah' by Plain White T's and 'Elvis Ain't Dead' by Scouting for Girls .

a) 4; b)3; c)5; d)1; e)2

PAGES 16 – 17
1. Niall's sign is Virgo - C
2. Liam's sign is Virgo - C
3. Louis' sign is Capricorn - B
4. Harry's sign is Aquarius - A
5. Zayn's sign is Capricorn – B

PAGES 18 – 19
A. Harry
B. Liam
C. Louis
D. Niall
E. Zayn

PAGES 20 – 21
1. 'What Makes You Beautiful'
Baby, you light up my world like nobody else.

2. 'One Thing'
So get out, get out, get out of my head.

3. 'Gotta Be You'
Oh and if you walk away I know I'll fade.

4. 'Gotta Be You'
'Cause there is nobody else.

5. 'One Thing'
I don't, I don't, don't know what it is.

6. 'One Thing'
And fall into my arms instead.

7. 'What Makes You Beautiful'
The way that you flip your hair gets me overwhelmed.

8. 'One Thing'
But I need that one thing and you've got that one thing.

9. 'What Makes You Beautiful'
But when you smile at the ground it ain't hard to tell.

10. 'What Makes You Beautiful'
You don't know, oh oh, you don't know you're beautiful.

PAGES 22 – 23
Niall   Zayn
Harry   Louis and Harry
Liam

1.E; 2.A; 3.D ;4.C ; 5.B

Person A is Zayn
Person B is Harry
Person C is Louis
Person D is Niall
Person E is Liam

PAGES 24 – 25
1. Liam's mouth
2. Harry's nose
3. Zayn's eye
4. Louis' chin
5. Liam's brows
6. Niall's nose
7. Louis' eye
8. Zayn's ear
9. Niall's eye
10. Harry's cheek

PAGES 26 – 27

"When I was little I always said I wanted a brother. Now it's like having four of them." Liam

"The doll came out when I had dodgy hair, so I made them take another scan so it looked better." Louis

"I'm a massive softy." Liam

"We've been to laser quest and we've said we want to go one further and go paintballing. That's good fun." Louis

"I was starstruck by Michelle Obama. She's an amazing looking lady, and I'm a massive Barack Obama fan anyway." Niall

"I think that Pigs in Blankets shouldn't just be limited to Christmas, they should be an all year round kind of thing." Harry

"Louis and I were outside and Louis saw a pigeon, so he ran to it and screamed 'Kevin? Is that you?'" Zayn

"I have four boyfriends!" Zayn

"I like girls who eat carrots." Louis

"Our stylist wants me to do a shoot in a mankini! I'm up for that." Harry

"Sometimes I see photos and think, I do have quite a lot of hair." Harry

"If you listen to Ed Sheeran's album, you'll know that he is one of the best lyricists I've ever heard in my life. He knows how to string words together like you wouldn't imagine. We were very lucky to work with him." Niall

PAGES 28 – 29
1. Zayn
2. Louis
3. Harry
4. Liam
5. Niall

(Quick Critter Quiz)
1. Niall
2. Koalas
3. Niall
4. His little sisters called the family's pet hamster after Louis' girlfriend Eleanor
5. Louis
6. One of his turtles chewed the leg of the other
7. Zayn
8. Harry

PAGES 30 – 31

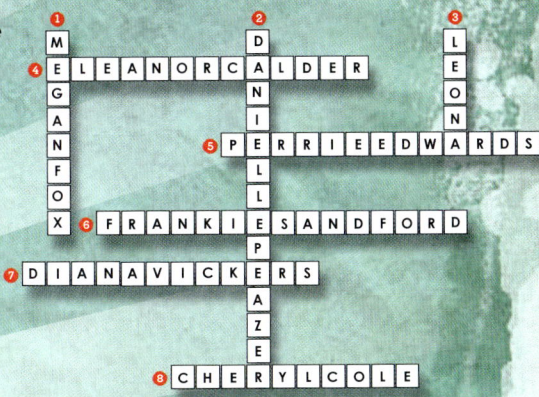

1. MEGANFOXX
2. DINILLPPAZE
3. LEON
4. ELEANORCALDER
5. PERRIEEDWARDS
6. FRANKIESANDFORD
7. DIANAVICKERS
8. CHERYLCOLE

PAGES 32 – 33
1. 1
2. 3
3. 15
4. 28
5. 35
6. 100 million
7. 60
8. 181
9. 60,000
10. 153,000
11. 5 million
12. 1,500,000

PAGES 34 – 35
1; 3; 6; 8; 9;

PAGES 38 – 39
Funny tee – worn by Harry
Comic clothing – worn by Liam
Brace yourself – worn by Louis
Onesies rule – worn by Harry
Many hatty returns – worn by Niall
70s vibe – worn by Niall
Dickie bow – worn by Harry
Granny knit – worn by Louis
Baseball jacket – worn by Zayn
Lovely lapels – worn by Liam

PAGES 40 - 41
Man bags, patterned tights, wellies with shorts, head to toe denim and kilts are unlikely to make it into the 1D wardrobe.

(Shoe Who)
Louis loves Toms
Harry loves Supra trainers

PAGES 42 – 43
(Venues of the World)
1. The O2 — DUBLIN
2. Motoropoint Arena — CARDIFF
3. HMV Hammersmith Apollo — LONDON
4. National indoor Arena — BIRMINGHAM
5. Echo Arena — LIVERPOOL

(Dream Destinations)
Sydney
Melbourne
Auckland
Toronto
Mexico City
Las Vegas
San Diego
Los Angeles
Orlando

(Opening Acts)
Boyce Avenue and Olly Murs

PAGES 44 – 45
1. Louis wore reindeer slippers – SURE DID
2. Niall shaved his own nipples - NAH, NEVER – it was Zayn who shaved his nipples
3. Security found a fan in a bin – SURE DID
4. Zayn got a mic tattoo – SURE DID
5. Niall hurt his thumb – SURE DID
6. Harry ran about in his boxers – SURE DID
7. Three of the lads got whiplash – SURE DID
8. Niall fainted after meeting the Obamas – NAH, NEVER
9. Liam caught a shark – SURE DID
10. Harry dyed Niall's hair red – NAH, NEVER
11. A man tried to get into Louis' hotel room – SURE DID
12. Louis stepped on Niall's hairbrush – NAH, NEVER
13. Harry challenged Biebz to a duel – NAH, NEVER
14. Louis bungee jumped – SURE DID

PAGES 46 – 47
"Niall's a bit crazy…." ZAYN
"On the plane, Harry got up…" LIAM
"My first real crush…" HARRY
"Zayn and me are Captain…" LOUIS
"At bootcamp, Liam was quite different…" NIALL

(Bromance)
Liam and Niall are often called… NIAM
Harry and Louis are often called… LARRY STYLINSON

PAGES 48 – 49

Z	Q	M	K	G	R	W	E	N	Y	A	P
T	H	A	R	R	Y	N	L	X	Y	I	P
W	I	O	A	K	J	U	F	R	E	D	U
X	V	R	I	T	T	S	S	I	U	O	X
L	N	I	H	O	R	A	N	X	U	I	A
X	A	S	I	M	T	V	J	N	F	A	C
M	H	G	N	L	E	D	O	W	U	M	L
Q	K	H	P	I	Y	M	D	P	B	X	L
N	O	D	W	N	I	Q	U	M	R	E	E
S	Y	V	X	S	T	Y	L	E	S	V	W
K	Y	A	M	O	T	N	S	W	M	T	O
E	T	X	Z	N	A	I	L	L	G	I	C

(Think you're done…)
Simon Cowell

PAGES 50 – 51
Liam and Louis
Harry and Zayn

PAGES 54 – 55
1. 'What Makes You Beautiful'
2. 'Gotta Be You'
3. 'One Thing'
4. 'More Than This'
5. 'What Makes You Beautiful'

6. 'Gotta Be You'
7. 'Gotta Be You'
8. 'One Thing'
9. 'Gotta Be You'
10. 'What Makes You Beautiful'
11. 'One Thing'
12. 'More Than This'

PAGES 56 – 57
(Prank-Stars)
1. Zayn
2. Drinking straws
3. Liam
4. Niall
5. Niall
6. He posted pix of himself with purple hair, pretending he'd dyed it, when it was only a toning and conditioning treatment
7. Put his hand on Simon's bottom
8. Liam
9. Harry
10. They got a producer to pretend she was in labour

PAGES 58 – 59

PAGES 60 – 61
1. True
2. False – he's the youngest
3. False – he sang 'Isn't She Lovely' by Stevie Wonder
4. True
5. True
6. False – he's from Cheshire

7. True
8. False – he has Ophidiophobia – a fear of snakes

PAGES 62 – 63
NA NA NA - HATE; BRAKES; SAY; CRAWLING; STAY
MORE THAN THIS – BROKEN; HEAR; BLINDED; EVERYTHING; DANCING; HEART; TURN
FOREVER YOUNG – DANCE; WHILE; WAIT; WATCHING; EXPECTING; DROP; BOMB TAKEN, - HAVE; SUDDENLY; SOMEBODY; WANT; SLEPT; ONE; MOVED ON; MISSED; ALONG

PAGES 64 - 65
'Stereo Hearts' by Gym Class Heroes
'Valerie' by The Zutons
'Torn' by Natalie Imbruglia
'Use Somebody' by Kings of Leon.
'I Gotta Feeling' by The Black Eyed Peas

They've not yet appeared on the cover of *Grazia*.

PAGES 66 – 67
1. False – he's 5ft 9
2. True
3. True
4. True
5. False – although he once spoke French in an interview
6. True
7. False – that belongs to Zayn. Louis is not a fan of tattoos
8. False – his birthday is on Christmas Eve

PAGES 68 – 69
1. Clasping them together
2. Louis
3. Two, Harry and Zayn
4. It's done up
5. Two
6. E 1
7. Spots (polka dots)
8. Harry
9. Inside a camper van
10. Orange and yellow checks

PAGES 72 – 73
1. True
2. False – he's from Pakistan
3. True
4. True
5. True – the visit to the judge's houses in Spain was his first time abroad
6. False – that's Liam's fave scent. Zayn loves *Unforgivable* by Sean John
7. True
8. False, that was Harry's band.

PAGES 74 – 75
1. 6a Justin Bieber
2. 2b Tom Parker of The Wanted
3. 5c James Maslow of Big Time Rush
4. 7d Miranda Cosgrove of *iCarly*
5. 3e Joe Jonas
6. 1f Olly Murs
7. 4g Simon Cowell

PAGES 76 – 77
Ted – I belong to Louis
Dusty – I belong to Harry

PAGES 78 – 79
1. False – he has only one kidney
2. False – he like Armani boxers
3. True
4. True
5. False – it's purple
6. False – he was studying music technology
7. False – he loves the Toy Story movies
8. True

PAGES 82 – 83
1. Courtside tickets to a basketball match – the Knicks v. the Toronto Raptors
2. Dynamo, real name Steven Frayne
3. A basketball half-court
4. Football
5. Surfing and Bungee Jumping
6. Justin Bieber
7. Liam
8. Three – Harry, Louis and Zayn
9. Skiing
10. Michael Jordan
11. A skateboard
12. The Olympics

PAGES 84 – 85
STAN- Louis   SCOTT - Niall   JOHN - Harry
ROB - Louis   RONNIE - Liam   DANNY - Zayn
CURTIS - Louis MARTIN - Liam   ANTHONY - Zay
BRAD- Niall   ANDY - Liam   AQUIB - Zayn
DILLAN- Niall BEN - Harry
SEAN - Niall   NICK - Harry

PAGES 86 – 87

PAGES 88 – 89
1. False – he's not a fan and has previously called them 'a turn off'
2. True
3. True – a present from Harry
4. True
5. True
6. True
7. False – Louis once sleepwalked into Niall's bed and started singing the Jungle Book song
8. False – he likes being on his own

PAGES 90 – 91
Chain A is Liam
Chain B is Zayn
Chain C is Louis

PAGES 92 – 93
1. Status Single
2. Invisibility
3. 'It Wasn't Me' by Shaggy
4. *Red and Black*
5. Niall
6. 10 minutes